2/94 Carolrhoda 1495/1121

D0475285

U
641.1 NOT
Nottridge, Rhoda.
Additives

1495

MAR -2 '96	DATE DUE	
DEC -2 '96		
JAN 3 0 '98		

Basalt Regional Library
P.O. Box BB
Basalt, CO 81621
927-4311

Additives

by Rhoda Nottridge

![colophon] Carolrhoda Books, Inc./Minneapolis

Basalt Regional Library
P. O. Box BB
Basalt, Colo. 81621

Words that appear in **bold** are explained in the glossary on page 30.

Illustrations by John Yates.
Cartoons by Maureen Jackson.

This book is available in two editions.
Library binding by Carolrhoda Books, Inc.
Soft cover by First Avenue Editions
241 First Avenue North
Minneapolis, Minnesota 55401

First published in the U.S. in 1993 by Carolrhoda Books, Inc.

All U.S. rights reserved. No part of this book may be reproduced or transmitted in any form or by any means, electronic or mechanical, including photocopying and recording, or by any information storage or retrieval system, without the prior written permission of Carolrhoda Books, Inc., except for the inclusion of brief quotations in an acknowledged review.

Copyright © 1992 Wayland (Publishers) Ltd., Hove, East Sussex. First published 1992 by Wayland (Publishers) Ltd.

Library of Congress Cataloging-in-Publication Data

Nottridge, Rhoda.
    Additives / by Rhoda Nottridge.
        p.   cm.
    Includes index.
    Summary: Focuses on food additives, discussing the different kinds, their uses, and whether they are harmful. Includes recipes and activities.
    ISBN 0-87614-794-5 (lib. bdg.)
    ISBN 0-87614-609-4 (pbk.)
    1. Food additives—Juvenile literature. 2. Food additives—Experiments—Juvenile literature.
[1. Food additives.] I. Title.
TX553.A3N65   1993
664'.04—dc20   92-33083
                                                                   CIP
                                                                    AC

Printed in Belgium by Casterman S.A.
Bound in the United States of America

1 2 3 4 5 6 98 97 96 95 94 93

Contents

What Are Additives?

Since ancient times, people have added vinegar, salt, or sugar to food to keep it from rotting. When people couldn't get fresh food, they used their supplies of preserved foods to keep them going through hard times.

Today, the things we use to preserve foods are called **additives.** Additives can be natural, such as salt, or artificial, such as those made from chemicals. We don't normally eat additives by themselves for food. They

BELOW *In the 1800s, meat was preserved in huge vats.*

are an addition, which is why we call them additives.

Along with preserving food, additives can make food look, taste, or feel different. This is not a new idea. The ancient Romans added natural soda to their vegetables to make them more colorful. They also tried to make bread that looked white instead of its natural brown color.

In the 1700s, so many people wanted white bread that bakers added dried, ground-up bones, chalk, and even poisonous white lead. These additives helped make brown bread look whiter. Adding lead to bread may sound ridiculous to us, but the idea of changing how a food looks, tastes, feels, and smells is more popular now than ever before.

Processed Foods

Making additives is a big business. Hundreds of new additives made from chemicals have been created in the last thirty years. Many of these additives go into making **processed foods.**

More than half of the food we buy is processed before we eat it. We do some of this processing ourselves. For example, we don't eat our potatoes raw. We bake, boil, or fry them, sometimes peeling them or adding salt to them first. However, most processing of food is done before food reaches the grocery store.

Why is so much of our food processed? Nowadays most people live in large towns or cities, far from where food is grown. Few people grow their own food. They buy food in stores.

Processing food helps it stay fresh longer in the store and at home. Less food is wasted, and people don't have to shop as often since food lasts longer. And even if a food only grows in one country during one season

of the year, people can enjoy it year-round if it is canned, dried, or processed in some other way.

BELOW
Additives give this processed dessert artificial strawberry flavor and color.

Investigating processed foods

You can find out for yourself how food processing has made it possible for people to eat a greater variety of food all year round. Next time you go shopping, take a closer look at the labels on the food you buy. Where does the food come from? Does the label tell you that this is a processed food? What is the date by which the product must be sold? Write down the answers in a notebook. Use a chart like the one below.

How many items in your shopping cart have been processed to help them travel and stay fresh longer?

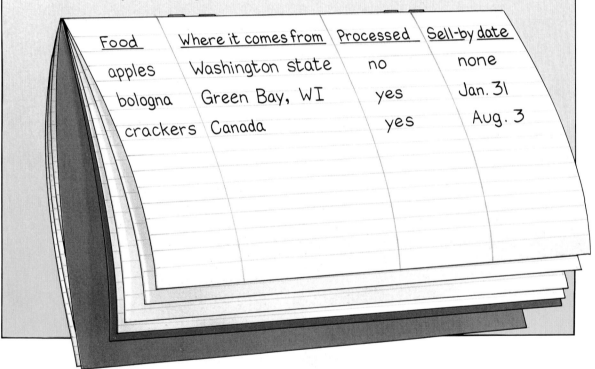

Food	Where it comes from	Processed	Sell-by date
apples	Washington state	no	none
bologna	Green Bay, WI	yes	Jan. 31
crackers	Canada	yes	Aug. 3

Although processing helps preserve foods, it also destroys some vitamins and minerals. In some processed foods, the lost vitamins and minerals aren't replaced. New, less healthy ingredients may be added instead. The more food is processed, the more likely it is to contain some of the many different additives.

People who make food are always trying to invent new products that look, taste, and feel different. More than half the food on the shelves at the grocery store didn't exist only ten years ago. These new products have sometimes been processed so much that little food value is left in them. They may also contain too much sugar, starch, and fat to be healthy.

Additives in processed food can create an artificial flavor, color, and taste. By using additives, something can be made to smell, taste, and look like a certain food without actually containing any of it.

Over 3,000 different kinds of additives are now in use. Some experts think that twice as many additives will be used in processed foods by the 21st century.

The most important types of additives used are preservatives, **antioxidants, emulsifiers, stabilizers,** flavorings, and colorings. They are used to change the look, feel, taste, and texture of food. Let's look at each of these types of additives in more detail and find out what they do.

Cooking experiment

Carry out your own experiment to see how additives are used to change the look, feel, and taste of food. By making two different batches of cake, you'll see how the different ingredients change the cake. To save time, ask a friend to mix up one batch while you do the other. Be sure an adult is present when you are cooking.

Ingredients for batch 1
(with additives)

¾ cup self-raising flour
½ teaspoon baking powder
½ teaspoon salt
1 cup white sugar
½ cup margarine, melted
⅔ cup milk
1 teaspoon vanilla extract
2 eggs
2 squares melted,
   unsweetened chocolate

Ingredients for batch 2
(without additives)

¾ cup plain flour
1 cup white sugar
½ cup margarine
⅔ cup milk
2 eggs

Instructions
For each recipe, mix the flour and other dry ingredients in a bowl. Add the rest of the ingredients, except for the eggs and the melted chocolate in batch 1. Beat well for two minutes. Add the remaining ingredients and beat for one minute. Pour the mixtures into greased, round cake pans and bake in an oven for about 45 minutes at 350°.

Results
Look at the two finished cakes. What are the differences between them? How did the additives affect the look, taste, and feel of the cakes?

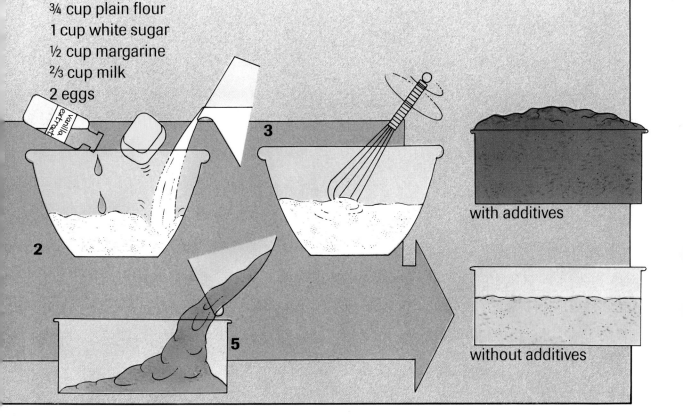

with additives

without additives

Preservatives and Antioxidants

ABOVE *One way to keep fruit from rotting is to preserve it by canning.*

Preservatives are probably the most important additives, because they help keep food fresh. Adding preservatives helps stop food from decaying and going bad.

Preservatives prevent molds and bacteria from growing. This means that food can be kept in grocery stores or at home for a long time.

Some preservatives are acids found naturally in fruit. Natural preservatives are used to preserve many things, such as sauces, pickles, and even some canned baby foods.

Antioxidants

An antioxidant is an additive that helps stop food from decaying when it's exposed to oxygen. We all need oxygen to live and breathe. But in addition to keeping us alive, oxygen makes things decay. Without oxygen, the bacteria that cause food to decay cannot work. Antioxidants protect food from coming into contact with oxygen.

If you cut a slice of apple and leave it out for a while, it begins to turn brown because of oxygen in the air. However, if you squeeze some lemon juice over the slice of apple, it will not change color. This is because lemon juice contains natural antioxidants called citric acid and ascorbic acid.

Chemical antioxidants are added to many oily foods to keep the oil from going bad.

Antioxidants such as **BHA** and **BHT** are added to many foods, from peanut butter to margarine to salad dressings.

But while antioxidants help preserve foods, some are poisonous in large amounts. Others may cause cancer.

Even natural antioxidants like citric acid can cause tooth decay and cavities. Antioxidants are generally used in food in very small amounts because scientists are not certain of their effects on people.

BELOW *Which apple slices have been preserved with lemon juice?*

Bananas, apples, and air

You can see for yourself how oxygen in the air works on food. For this experiment, you will need colored crayons, paper, an apple, and a banana. Leave the apple and banana in a dish for a few days. Each day, draw all the changes you see. Did the skins wrinkle or turn color? Which fruit went bad first? What other changes did you see?

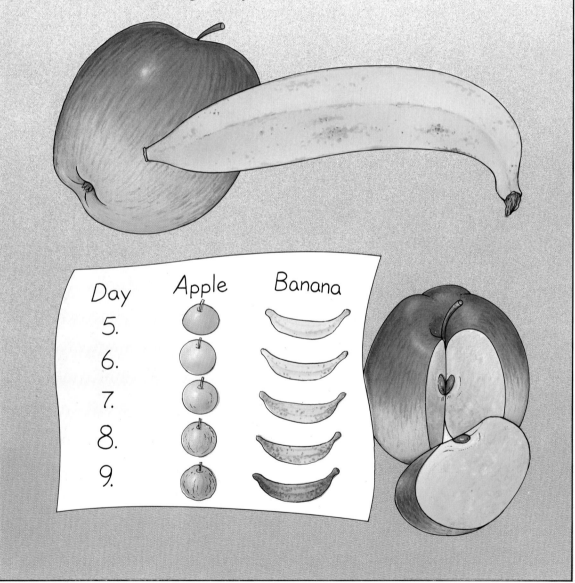

Emulsifiers, Stabilizers, and Thickeners

Some additives change a food's texture. These are called emulsifiers, stabilizers, and thickeners.

Oil and water normally separate when they are mixed together. Foods like margarine, salad dressing, and cocoa are made using both oil and water. Emulsifiers stop these ingredients from separating. Once an emulsifier has been used, a stabilizer is often added to stop ingredients from separating again.

While emulsifiers and stabilizers keep ingredients together, thickeners are added to thicken pudding, yogurt, and other foods. Many thickeners, emulsifiers, and stabilizers come from natural things such as eggs, tree saps, seaweeds, and wood pulp. But many others are made from combining chemicals. Their names—polysorbates and propylene glycol—can be hard to pronounce, but they act just like natural additives.

BELOW *Sap from the acacia tree is used as a natural thickener in food.*

Make your own emulsifier mayonnaise

Recipe
This recipe for mayonnaise uses an egg yolk as a natural emulsifier. The yolk binds together ingredients that would normally separate.

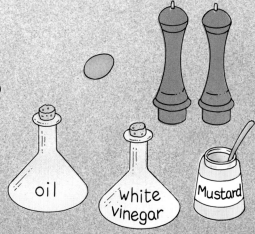

Ingredients
1 egg, just the yolk
1 teaspoon mustard
¾ cup salad oil
vinegar or lemon juice
salt and pepper

Equipment
teaspoon
measuring cup
bowl
hand whisk

Instructions
1. Put the egg yolk, mustard, salt, and pepper in a bowl and let sit.
2. Pour the oil into a measuring cup. 3. Then mix the egg yolk and mustard together with the whisk. 4. Add a drop of oil to the egg mixture and beat it in well with the whisk. Add more oil, being sure to mix it in well. Try not to pour in too much oil at once or the mixture won't thicken. Continue to add the oil drop by drop until it's all used up. 5. Stir in a scant teaspoonful of vinegar or lemon juice until the mixture is smooth.

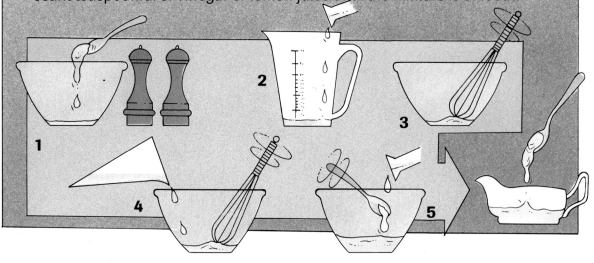

Colorings

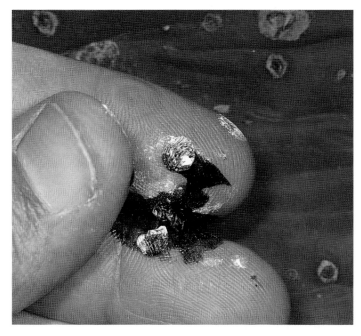

Coloring food to make it look nicer is not a new idea. Some of the food colorings we use have been additives for many centuries. For example, cochineal is a red coloring found in Central American beetles. Hundreds of years ago, the Aztecs crushed the beetles to use as a coloring. We still use cochineal to color some foods.

Cochineal is a natural food coloring, but about 95 percent of colorings now used are artificial. Food colorings usually have no food value. They are used only to make food look different or more appealing. They are sometimes listed on labels by their dye number, as in "Yellow No. 5."

Some food dyes and colors used in the past have been found to be quite dangerous. In the 1800s, colorings containing poisons such as mercury, lead, and copper were commonly used. Governments around the world realized that they would have to stop food manufacturers from using certain food colorings.

In the United States, the **Food and Drug Administration,** or FDA, is in charge of deciding which colorings and other additives can be used. The FDA, however, does not test each additive for safety. Instead, manufacturers must test food colorings and other additives they want to use. They can also ask an outside laboratory to do the tests for them. Test results go to the FDA, which decides if the additive is safe.

People have become ill from eating foods with

ABOVE *This cochineal beetle has been crushed to show the red dye inside.*

certain additives, especially artificial colorings. Children and babies are most at risk, because their bodies are smaller. Some artificial food colorings have been banned, and food manufacturers are trying to find safer, more natural colorings to use in their place.

Although some food colorings cause health problems, colorings also have some important benefits. We expect a certain food to have a particular color. For example, we would expect a banana to be yellow. However, the color of food often changes if it is left in strong light or heat. When food is canned, heat changes its natural colors. Both strawberries and peas turn brown when they are canned. Colorings are added to make these foods look more natural and appetizing.

ABOVE *Which of these foods doesn't contain any coloring? If you guessed the sugar, you guessed right.*

A candy maker once carried out an experiment that helps explain why certain foods need colorings. The candy maker made candies shaped like different fruit. There were yellow banana-shaped candies, green apple-shaped ones, and other fruit shapes. But while the candies looked like one fruit, they tasted like another. Candies that looked like oranges, for example, tasted like lemons.

Very few of the people given the candies could guess what flavor they were eating. They expected yellow banana-shaped candy to taste like bananas, and orange-shaped candy to taste like

What does it taste like?

You can carry out your own version of the candy maker's test. For this experiment, you'll need orange and yellow food coloring and lemon and orange flavoring. You'll also need to whip up some quick, homemade candy. Use a wire whisk to mix together an egg white and 1 and ⅓ cups of powdered sugar. Once it's mixed, divide the candy batter into two bowls. Add orange food coloring and lemon flavoring to one bowl. Add yellow food coloring and orange flavoring to the other. Mix until both are evenly colored. Then put spoonfuls of the candy onto waxed paper to harden.

Once the candies are ready, try them out on your friends. Don't tell them what the flavors are. Can they guess the flavors correctly? If not, why do you think they guessed wrong?

oranges. This suggests that we connect the taste of a food with a particular color.

Things such as popsicles and soft drinks are often given colorings because they would otherwise look pale. Adding color makes them brighter and more attractive.

Colorings are even used to change the color of food before it is produced. When chickens are allowed to roam around in a barnyard, eating a lot of different foods, they produce eggs with a golden-colored yolk. Eggs from free-range chickens are affected by foods chickens eat.

Hens laying eggs at large-scale egg farms are not allowed to range freely. They are kept in cages all the time. The grains they eat may not contain the natural colors that produce golden yolks.

Egg yolk colors can vary from pale yellow to deep orange. But large-scale egg farmers add red or yellow colorings to the chicken feed in order to control the egg yolk color. These dyes change the color of the egg yolks, so that they will be the color people expect. The rich golden-yellow color of the eggs we eat is often just an

added coloring.

It is often difficult to know whether colorings or dyes have been added to animal feed. In the United States, information about colors added to feed is often printed on the egg carton.

Many countries allow only certain colorings to be used. This varies around the world. Norway does not allow any artificial colors in food, while Great Britain allows 16. In the United States, the FDA has a list of certified colors now in use. New colors must pass tests to be certified.

ABOVE *Yolks in eggs laid by hens in poultry farms aren't as golden yellow as yolks in free-range eggs.*

Flavorings and Enhancers

More than 2,000 different flavorings are used in food processing. Flavorings are the most common additives and may be natural or artificial.

Flavorings are often made up of a huge number of chemicals and other ingredients. However, food manufacturers don't have to list all the chemicals used. They simply list the flavoring as "real," "natural," or "artificial" on the label.

A product described as having "raspberry flavor" may not have any natural raspberry in it at all. It may only contain artificial raspberry flavoring made from chemicals.

Many natural and artificial flavorings have never been tested. Some were in use before the FDA began regulating additives. Because they have been used for

BELOW *Many candies are flavored artificially with chemicals.*

Natural banana shakes

This tasty recipe for banana milkshakes uses only natural ingredients. The natural flavor comes from the bananas.

Ingredients
2 cups milk
2 or 3 bananas,
 sliced

Equipment
large bowl
whisk or blender
2 tall glasses

Instructions
Mash the bananas in the bowl using a fork. Add the milk and whisk slowly until the mixture is smooth and frothy. If you're using a blender, put all the ingredients into the machine and blend for one minute, or until the mixture is smooth and frothy. Pour the milkshakes into two tall glasses.

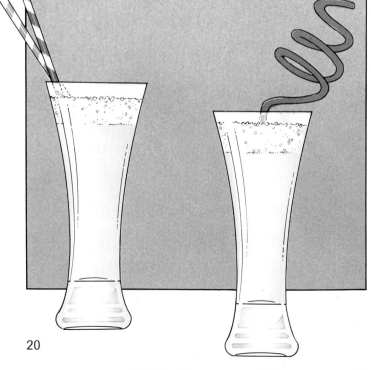

many years without causing any problems that we know of, the FDA has put them on a list called "generally recognized as safe," or **GRAS.**

Flavorings are only used in very tiny amounts. The amount added is often about 1,000 times smaller than the amount of preservatives used.

Flavor enhancers
A **flavor enhancer** is not a flavoring. It makes the flavor already in food taste stronger.

Flavor enhancers aren't new. For many years, Japanese cooks added the water in which they had cooked a type of seaweed to other foods. Something in the seaweed, which didn't taste of anything on its own, made other things taste good.

This flavor enhancer, called **monosodium glutamate** or MSG, is often used in Asian cooking. It can be made from sugar beets, corn, and other substances. Nowadays, MSG is used in processed foods, from instant soups to potato chips.

MSG makes food taste good, but it can cause problems. Large amounts of it have caused brain damage in animals. For this reason,

MSG is not used in baby food in the United States.

For most people, eating MSG in small amounts in food will not cause any ill effects. Some people, however, feel that flavor enhancers spoil the sense of taste. When we become used to stronger flavors, our taste buds become less sensitive.

Sweet additions

Most processed foods contain sweeteners. Most sweeteners are made from sugar, but many others are artificial sugar substitutes. Additives made from sugar include brown sugar, honey, corn syrup, and sugars ending in -ose, like dextrose and glucose.

Sugar substitutes such as saccharine and aspartame make food taste sweet but contain no natural sugars. Saccharine was on the GRAS list until tests linked it to cancer. Now all foods containing saccharine must carry a warning label.

ABOVE
Monosodium glutamate, or MSG, can be made from wheat as well as from seaweed.

How Safe Are Additives?

Even after an additive has passed 100 tests, there is no guarantee that it will pass its 101st test. Food manufacturers must use animals when they test new additives. But humans and animals don't always react to additives in the same way. And most people don't live in an environment that is as clean as a food-testing laboratory.

Food for thought

In New York, an experiment was carried out to see how additives affect children's

Americans eat an average of 150 pounds of additives every year. Most people notice no bad effects from the additives they eat. However, some people have allergic reactions after eating. They will wonder if additives were the cause. Because many people are allergic to certain foods, such as strawberries, milk, or shellfish, it's often hard to know whether the additives in food or the food itself caused the problem.

Additives are constantly being tested for safety. But we can't be completely sure that an additive is safe.

ABOVE *These foods contain no additives, yet some people are allergic to them.*

schoolwork. Almost a million children joined in the experiment.

School lunches in New York at that time contained many additives. In the experiment, meals were changed and the number of additives was reduced. When the children ate these new meals, their test scores went up over 15 percent.

We cannot be sure that eating fewer additives will improve your grades. But wholesome food at the schools in the New York experiment seemed to help kids work better.

If you want to know how or if additives affect you, try running your own experiment. After each meal, write down what you've eaten. Look at the labels of any processed foods to see what additives were used. Then watch yourself to see how you act and feel. Write down your reactions.

BELOW *This meal is made from fresh food with no additives.*

Avoiding Additives

Better health and taste are not the only reasons for avoiding additives. Some additives are made from dairy or animal products, which some **vegetarians** and other people do not eat.

Hidden additives

Not all additives are easy to avoid. Some aren't listed on food labels because they are used early in the stages of food production. Pesticides, for example, are applied while the food is growing to keep it free of bugs. Pesticides are sprayed on almost all fruit, nuts, and vegetables. When we eat these foods, some of the chemicals sprayed on them often remain.

Hormones are another kind of hidden additive. Many animals are fed hormones when they are young to speed up their growth. While farmers generally stop using hormones long before the animals are killed, some hormones may remain in the meat.

It isn't always possible to know whether growth hormones or pesticides have been used. Some stores label meats in which no growth hormones have been used.

One way to avoid additives such as pesticides is to wash fruit and vegetables thoroughly. To avoid them altogether, look for **organic** fruit, nuts, vegetables, and other foods. When crops are grown organically, no pesticides or other chemicals are used.

BELOW *Spraying fruit trees with pesticides stops insects from destroying fruit.*

Be an Additive Detective

The first and best place to look for clues about additives is right on the package. Nearly all processed foods list the ingredients used on the label.

The ingredients normally are listed in order of the amount used, from most to least. The amount is measured by weight.

If, for example, salt is high on the list of ingredients for a can of baked beans, you can be sure that a lot of salt was added. Additives tend to be near the end of the list because they are used in tiny amounts and don't weigh very much.

How to read a label

Over half of all Americans read the labels of the foods they buy. The information on labels can be difficult to understand or even misleading.

Some food labels don't list ingredients at all, but they are the exceptions to the rule. These foods, such as pasta, soft drinks, and jellies, are made from standard

or traditional recipes. Ingredients may be listed on the label, but the law doesn't require it.

Even on food labels listing ingredients, not all additives have to be listed. Additives on the GRAS list, for example, are not required on the label.

Even though labels may be incomplete, they do offer

ABOVE *Take time to read the ingredients carefully next time you go to the store.*

RIGHT *Most products have a list of ingredients on the label.*

useful information. Here, for example, are the ingredients from a box of crackers: enriched flour, sugar, dextrose, coconut oil (contains citric acid), salt, sodium bicarbonate.

Look at the ingredients from the beginning. The word *enriched* tells you that vitamins and minerals destroyed during processing have been put back in. *Dextrose*, ending in -ose, is a sweetener. The citric acid in the coconut oil is a natural preservative. *Sodium bicarbonate* looks like a strange chemical additive, but the dictionary will tell you that it's just another name for baking soda, which makes baked foods rise.

Is this food good for you? Take another look at the label and see how the ingredients add up. Both sugar and dextrose are high on the list. Since ingredients are listed by weight, you can guess that these crackers are sugary.

Should you eat them? That's a choice you must make for yourself.

Know your additives

You can investigate for yourself which brands of food contain more additives by comparing labels. You'll need a pen, some paper, and two different brands of your favorite food. Write down on your paper the list of ingredients for each brand. Do both brands contain the same ingredients? Does one have more of a certain ingredient than the other? (Remember, ingredients are listed in order of the amount used.) Which brand do you think is more healthy? Why?

Ingredients: beef stock, carrots, potatoes, cooked beef, tomatoes, corn, cornstarch, salt, hydrolyzed vegetable protein, caramel color, and natural flavors.

Ingredients: beef stock, beef, carrots, tomatoes with juice, potatoes, corn, tomato paste, salt, beef fat, pepper.

Making a Choice

How many additives do you want to have in your diet? You make choices about additives every time you eat food, sip drinks, and munch on snacks. You can buy foods with or without additives— just read the label.

BELOW
By shopping carefully, you can avoid foods with lots of additives.

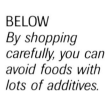

If you don't know what an ingredient is, look it up. The dictionary is a good place to start. For more in-depth information about additives and other ingredients, use the sources listed on page 31.

Look closely at food packages. Most will list the manufacturer's address. Write directly to the company if you have questions about additives in the product. Some manufacturers even list toll-free telephone numbers for questions, right on the food label.

It may take you a while to sort through the names of the ingredients, but by learning to read food labels carefully you will know which products contain less or no additives. Remember, if you don't make a choice about the additives you eat, that choice will be made for you by others.

The more you read about food and additives, the better choices you can make about the foods you eat. Careful eating will help you keep your mind sharp and your body healthy.

Glossary

additives Anything added to a food. Sugar, spices, and salt are natural additives. Many additives are artificial substances made from chemicals.

antioxidants Additives that stop oxygen in the air from causing foods to decay

BHA Short for butylated hydroxyanisole, this additive is an antioxidant. Along with **BHT,** short for butylated hydroxytoluene, BHA is used in many junk foods.

emulsifiers Additives that help keep ingredients from separating. Eggs are natural emulsifiers; mono- and diglycerides are artificial emulsifiers.

flavor enhancer An additive that makes the taste of a food more intense

Food and Drug Administration A part of the United States government that regulates the use of most food additives

GRAS A list of additives that can be used in food and do not have to be listed on labels. Because they have been in use for some time and have caused no known health problems, these additives are thought to be safe.

monosodium glutamate A flavor enhancer often shortened to MSG on food labels. This additive is used in many processed foods and can cause allergic reactions in some people.

organic A way of growing food without the use of fertilizers, pesticides, chemicals, or other hidden additives

processed foods Foods that have been changed before eating. Spreadable American cheese made from artificial and natural ingredients is just one example of a highly processed food.

stabilizers Substances such as gelatin that give foods a smooth and uniform texture and keep them from separating. Stabilizers are often used with emulsifiers.

vegetarians People who choose not to eat meat

Books to Read

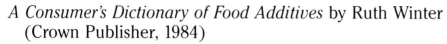

The Complete Eater's Digest & Nutrition Scoreboard by Dr. Michael Jacobson (Anchor Books, 1985)

A Consumer's Dictionary of Food Additives by Ruth Winter (Crown Publisher, 1984)

*Good for Me!: All About Food in 32 Bites by Marilyn Burns (Little Brown and Company, 1978)

*How Safe Is Our Food Supply? by J. McCoy (Franklin Watts, 1990)

*Vegetarian Cooking Around the World (Lerner Publications, 1992)

*for younger readers

Metric Chart

To find measurements that are almost equal

WHEN YOU KNOW:	MULTIPLY BY:	TO FIND:
AREA		
acres	0.41	hectares
WEIGHT		
ounces (oz.)	28.0	grams (g)
pounds (lb.)	0.45	kilograms (kg)
LENGTH		
inches (in.)	2.5	centimeters (cm)
feet (ft.)	30.0	centimeters
VOLUME		
teaspoons (tsp.)	5.0	milliliters (ml)
tablespoons (Tbsp.)	15.0	milliliters
fluid ounces (oz.)	30.0	milliliters
cups (c.)	0.24	liters (l)
quarts (qt.)	0.95	liters
TEMPERATURE		
Fahrenheit (°F)	0.56 (after subtracting 32)	Celsius (°C)

Basalt Regional Library
P. O. Box BB
Basalt, Colo. 81621

Index